Would You Rather?
Silly Questions for Kids
300+ Crazy Questions for Hours of Fun at Home and in the Classroom

Laughing Lion

Free **Audiobook versions** of this and many other Laughing Lion books?
Sign up using the link below or scan the QR code with your phone.

bit.ly/3j3vmD2

Hey there, brave wanderer!

Do you want to go on an adventure? Better yet, do you want to CREATE your own adventure? Grab your friends and ready your weapons, because this book is going to take you for a ride!

This book is a collection of Would You Rather questions that lead to magical and exciting choices. To play, take turns asking each other the questions for each chapter. Don't forget to explain WHY you picked your answer so that everyone can join in on the fun. The farther you journey into the book, the harder the questions will be, so do your best to answer all questions until the end!

This game is perfect for sleepovers, parties, and icebreakers to help everyone get to know each other better. Lastly, this game is especially made for the brave and adventurous, so if you're ready to embark on this new journey, go ahead and flip to the next pages!

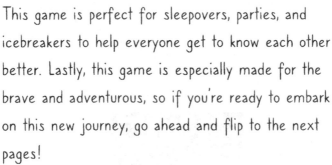

CONTENTS

CREATE YOUR CHARACTER FIRST

Let's choose your powers and talents!

Would you rather...

Be a MAGIC WIZARD

or

Be a SUPERHERO?

Have the power to READ MINDS

or

Have the power to BE INVISIBLE?

Run REALLY FAST

or

Be REALLY STRONG?

Be able to TALK TO ANIMALS

or

Have a BEAUTIFUL VOICE?

Be really good at MATH

or

Be really good at SPORTS?

Be able to GO BACK IN TIME

or

Be able to STOP TIME?

Be able to PLAY THE GUITAR?

or

Be able to PLAY THE PIANO?

Have WINGS to fly

or

Use a JETPACK?

Be super SMART

or

Be super LUCKY?

Be able BREATHE UNDER WATER

or

Be able to WALK ON WATER?

Have X-RAY VISION

or

SHOOT LASERS FROM YOUR EYES?

Be able to TELEPORT

or

Be able to TIME TRAVEL?

Understand SIGN LANGUAGE

or

Have the ability to LIP READ?

Have NIGHT VISION

or

Be able to SEE THE FUTURE?

Have the ability to FREEZE TIME

or

Have the ability to TURN INTO A TIGER?

Be the SUPERHERO

or

Be the EVIL VILLAIN?

Only be able to WHISPER

or

Only be able to SHOUT?

Be really TALL

or

Really STRONG?

Shoot FIRE from your hands

or

Breathe ICE?

Be able to talk to PLANTS

or

Be able to FLY?

Have a remote control that can FAST FORWARD your life

or

A remote control that can REWIND it?

The ability to SEE THROUGH WALLS

or

The ability to WALK THROUGH WALLS?

Turn anything you touch to GOLD

or

Turn it into DIAMONDS?

Be able to UNDERSTAND ANIMALS

or

READ PEOPLE'S MINDS?

Be able to FIND ANYTHING LOST

or

Make anyone TELL THE TRUTH whenever you TOUCH them?

Be able to CONTROL THE WEATHER

or

Be able to CONTROL TIME?

Be a FAMOUS EXPLORER

or

Be an UNKNOWN FOREST GUARDIAN?

WHERE ARE WE GOING?

Time to start CREATING your journey!

Would you rather...

Go to OUTER SPACE

or

Go INSIDE A VOLCANO?

Visit HOGWARTS

or

Visit NARNIA?

See people flying on ROCKET SHIPS

or

Make friends with ROBOTS?

Travel on A PIRATE SHIP

or

Travel on A PRIVATE AIRPLANE?

See FLYING CARS

or

Ride a CAR THAT CAN GO UNDER WATER?

Have a PET DINOSAUR

or

Have a PET DRAGON?

Meet the EASTER BUNNY

or

Meet SANTA CLAUS?

Be stranded on an ISLAND

or

Be stranded in a FOREST?

Find a MERMAID

or

Find a UNICORN?

Go on a MAGICAL MISSION in Disneyland

or

BATTLE MUMMIES near the Egyptian pyramids?

Find HIDDEN TREASURE

or

Discover A NEW PLANET?

Have a MAGIC FLYING CARPET

or

Your OWN PERSONAL ROBOT?

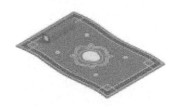

Play in the SAND

or

Play in the SNOW?

Find a flying UNICORN

or

Find a DRAGON?

Team up with the AVENGERS

Or the

JUSTICE LEAGUE?

Be friends with SPIDERMAN

or

Be friends with BATMAN?

Fly riding a BROOMSTICK

or

Fly on the back of a DRAGON?

Walk around wearing a WITCH'S HAT

or

Wear a VAMPIRE'S CAPE all day?

Cross the ocean on a SUBMARINE

or

Ride over it on a HELICOPTER?

Find a TIME MACHINE

or

Find a MAGIC WAND?

Meet a character in your FAVORITE BOOK

or

A character in your FAVORITE VIDEO GAME?

Have THREE FREE WISHES

or

Be the RICHEST PERSON in the world?

Live in a house made of GUMMY BEARS

or

A house made of MARSHMALLOWS?

Stay a week on THE NORTH POLE

or

Stay a week in HAWAII?

Live on a FARM with animals

or

Live beside a SUNNY BEACH?

Spend the day shoveling the SNOW

or

Raking the LEAVES?

A world with NO ELECTRICITY

or

A world with NO RUNNING WATER?

Live UNDER THE GROUND

or

Live UNDER WATER?

Live where you are FOR A YEAR

or

Move to a different country EVERY MONTH?

Live in a TREE-HOUSE forever

or

Live on a BOAT forever?

Do the DISHES in a royal palace?

or

Clean the TOILETS in a royal palace?

Own an ANIMAL RESCUE SHELTER

or

Own a ZOO?

Sleep over with princesses with NO PILLOW under your head

or

Sleep with SEVEN LAYERS OF BLANKETS?

Go exploring in a magic forest NAKED

or

Sleep for SIX MONTHS?

Build a palace beside a jungle full of MONKEYS

or

Beside a river full of CROCODILES?

Have a BIG YARD covered only in PLAIN GLASS

or

Have a SMALL YARD with a SWING SET?

Live in a fort made of BRANCHES

or

Live in a fort made of PILLOWS?

Get your own ROLLER COASTER,

or

Your own KID-SIZE TRAIN?

Sleep on a PILLOW that smells like fish

or

Have to wear CLOTHES that smell like fish?

Live in a house with a SMELLY BATHROOM

or

Live in a house with a SMELLY BEDROOM?

Take out the GARBAGE with bare hands

or

Wash the GARBAGE CAN with bare hands?

OUR ANIMAL FRIENDS

We can't forget about the animal friends we meet along the way!

Would you rather...

Pet a baby LION

or

Pet a baby ELEPHANT?

Be a DOG for ONE DAY

or

Be a CAT for ONE DAY?

See a GIANT MOUSE

or

See a TINY GIRAFFE?

Ride on the back of a GIRAFFE

or

Ride on the back of a HORSE?

Kiss a SEAHORSE

or

Step on a CRAB?

Catch SEVEN LITTLE FISH

or

Catch ONE REALLY BIG FISH?

Be a BIRD

or

Be a FISH?

Get a PUPPY

or

Get a KITTEN?

Have a PET SNAKE

or

Have a PET SPIDER?

Swim in the OCEAN with SHARKS

or

Be stuck in a CAGE with LIONS?

Swim with the DOLPHINS in the ocean

or

Fly with the BIRDS in the sky?

Live with a MONKEY on your back

or

Live with a SNAKE on your arm?

Have a pet KANGAROO

or

Have a pet KOALA?

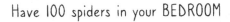

See a GIANT HAMSTER

or

See a TINY RHINO?

Have 100 spiders in your BEDROOM

or

Have 1 million ants in the rest of your HOUSE?

Feed a HORSE an apple

or

Give a CAMEL some water to drink?

Clean a CAT with your TONGUE

or

Be SPRAYED by a SKUNK?

Pet a poisonous SNAKE

or

Swim with an ELECTRIC EEL?

Have a PIG'S NOSE

or

CAT WHISKERS on your face?

Wake up with a GIRAFFE NECK

Or

an ELEPHANT TRUNK?

Have a pet TIGER

or

Have a pet ORANGUTAN?

Face a GIANT SNAIL

or

A GIANT GRASSHOPPER?

Stay in a city ruled by DOGS

or

A city ruled by CATS?

Have to MOO LIKE A COW before speaking

or

BARK LIKE A DOG before speaking?

Have BUTTERFLY WINGS

or

Have a HORSE TAIL?

Turn into a BEAR once a week

or

Turn into a BIRD once a week?

Sound like a MONKEY when you LAUGH

or

Sound like a ROOSTER when you CRY?

Be a SPIDER for a day

or

Be a MOSQUITO for a day?

Have a pet IGUANA

or

Have a pet TURTLE?

See a KOMODO DRAGON when walking to school

or

See a MOUNTAIN LION when walking to school?

Have a pet dog YOU CAN TALK TO

or

Have a pet dog that can DO YOUR CHORES?

See a CAT that BARKS

or

See a DOG that MEOWS?

Have a pet PARROT

Or

Have a pet MONKEY?

Stay in a treehouse full of SQUIRRELS

or

Full of RACCOONS?

Touch a CATERPILLAR

Or

Have a MOTH land in your eye?

BEWITCHED!

A witch throws a random magic potion at you!

Would you rather...

Always have an ITCH

or

Always have a COUGH?

Have four LEGS

or

Have four ARMS?

Have really BIG HANDS

or

Have really SMALL FEET?

Be sick for A WEEK

or

Get a SINGLE SHOT from the doctor?

Have a head the size of an APPLE

or

The size of a WATERMELON?

Lose all your HAIR

or

Lose all your TEETH?

Be so TALL your head hits the roof

or

So SHORT you can't reach the counter?

Wake up with a SQUIRREL'S TAIL

or

Wake up with a rabbit's nose

Have HAIR that goes past your KNEES

or

Be COMPLETELY BALD?

Grow GOAT HORNS

or

Grow BAT WINGS?

Have BLUE HAIR

or

Have RED EYES?

Be TEN INCHES tall

or

Be TEN FEET tall?

Have a DUCK'S BILL

or

Have a MONKEY'S FACE?

Never open your EYES

or

Never open your MOUTH?

Have only ONE BIG EYE

or

Have TWO NOSES?

Have an extra FINGER

or

Have an extra TOE?

Have a LONG FLUFFY TAIL

or

Have BIG ELF EARS?

Have green TEETH

or

Have green EYEBALLS?

Have PINK HAIR

or

Have PURPLE HAIR?

Have THREE ears

or

Only ONE ear?

Have an EAR where your NOSE is

or

NOSES where your EARS are?

Get THREE EYES

or

An EXTRA MOUTH?

Long EYELASHES that reach your cheeks

or

Long EYEBROWS that reach below your eyes?

A really big TUMMY

or

A really big BUTT?

Have CRUSTY EYES

or,

Have BAD BREATH?

Have a very LONG NECK

or

NO NECK at all?

Have FOUR eyebrows

or

NO eyebrows at all?

Walk around with MESSY HAIR

or

Walk around with MISMATCHED CLOTHES?

FAST-GROWING HAIR that needs to be cut every week

or

SLOW-GROWING HAIR that needs to be cut only after TEN YEARS?

Your DRINK always SPILLS

or

Your FOOD is always COLD?

Always wear a PINK FUZZY SWEATER

Or

Never be able to wear SHORTS?

Extra-long TEETH

Or

Extra-long FINGERS?

Be turned into a ROBOT

or

Be turned into a DOLL?

Grow OCTOPUS legs

or

CATERPILLAR legs?

Have dirty HANDS all the time

or

Have dirty FEET all the time?

Have your HANDS completely covered in hair

or

Have your NECK completely covered in hair?

Have a belly button on your FOREHEAD

or

Have a bellybutton on your CHIN?

Have A BIG PIMPLE in between your eyes

or

FIVE SMALL PIMPLES on your cheek?

YOUR FIRST QUEST

May we challenge you to a DARE?

Would you rather...

Spend a month feeling COLD all the time

or

Spend a month feeling HOT all the time?

Eat the SAME FOOD for ten years

or

Never watch YOUTUBE ever again?

Never get SICK ever again

or

Never have BAD DREAMS?

Get out of QUICKSAND

or

Jump into ICY WATER?

Win a CAR RACE

or

Learn to fly an AIRPLANE?

Smell ROTTEN EGGS

or

Smell your DAD'S SHOES?

Stay up really LATE

or

Wake up really EARLY?

LIE to your best friend

or

Tell your parents the TRUTH?

Not be able to SEE COLORS

or

Not be able to TASTE ANYTHING?

Never wear SHOES again

or

Never wear GLOVES again?

Have LOUD farts that smell GOOD

or

SILENT farts that smell TERRIBLE?

Find a cockroach in your PIZZA

or

Lots of angry ants inside your SHOE?

Brush your teeth with SHAMPOO

or

Brush your teeth with a bar of SOAP?

Never use the INTERNET again

or

Never watch TV again?

Give up your COMPUTER

or

Give up your PET?

Smell like stinky ARMPITS

or

Smell like FISH?

Hop like a KANGAROO everywhere

or

Walk slow like a TURTLE?

Wear a SWIMSUIT for the rest of your life

or

FORMAL WEAR for the rest of your life?

Have to always wear a thick SCARF

or

Have to always wear thick GLOVES?

Wear SHOES with laces that keep on getting UNTIED

or

Wear SOCKS that are always FALLING DOWN?

Have a finger coming out of your NOSE

or

Have it coming out of one EAR?

Eat COLD food all the time

or

Eat HOT food all the time?

Be shot out of a CANNON

or

Jump out of a PLANE?

Not be able to SPEAK for a year

or

Be BLIND instead?

Be an ONLY CHILD

or

The MIDDLE CHILD of seven children?

PLAN A FUN DAY!

Let's take a break from quests first and explore the land!

Would you rather...

Go to a land full of CHOCOLATE

or

Spend the day watching your FAVORITE MOVIES?

Go to the ZOO

or

Go to the WATERPARK?

Spend a day at the BEACH

or

Spend a day at the PARK?

Spend the morning playing INSIDE

or

Spend it playing OUTSIDE?

Play SOCCER

or

Play BASKETBALL?

Create a new SPORT

or

Create a new HOLIDAY?

See a FIREWORK SHOW

or

See a CIRCUS PERFORMANCE?

Play LASER TAG

or

Play PAINTBALL?

Ride a scary ROLLERCOASTER

or

Swim in the deep end of the POOL?

Spend three days in a CABIN IN THE WOODS

or

Spend three days in a FIVE-STAR HOTEL?

Go SKIING for the day

or

Go SNOWBOARDING?

Go SLEDDING on a COLD day

or

Go SWIMMING on a HOT day?

Jump into a POOL

or

Jump into a PILE OF LEAVES?

Read COMIC BOOKS

or

Play MINECRAFT?

Go to the MOVIES

or

Have a SLEEPOVER?

Watch a COMEDY movie

or

Watch a really SCARY movie?

Spend the day READING BOOKS

or

Spend it WRITING STORIES?

Have a WATER-BALLOON fight

or

Have a SNOWBALL fight?

Be on a SMALL BOAT

or

Be on a LARGE SHIP?

Go FISHING while playing with mermaids

or

Explore the FOREST guided by pixies?

Eat at all the RESTAURANTS you want

or

Buy all the TOYS you want?

Travel by AIRPLANES

or

Travel by HOT AIR BALLOON?

Go SNORKELING

or

Go KAYAKING?

Go SKYDIVING

or

Go BUNGEE JUMPING?

Take a LONG SHOWER

or

Take a BUBBLE BATH?

Eat BREAKFAST in a HOT AIR BALLOON

or

Eat DINNER inside a CASTLE?

Ride a ZIP-LINE

or

Ride a BIG WATERSLIDE?

Fly a KITE

Or

Ride a SKATEBOARD?

Play with LEGOS

or

PAINT a picture?

Play MONOPOLY

or

Play JENGA?

Watch your favorite MOVIE

or

Play your favorite VIDEO GAME?

Go on a HIKE barefoot

or

Go to the BEACH with a coat?

Swim in a huge swimming POOL

or

Swim in a small LAKE?

But ONE GREAT TOY that you can play with for FIVE YEARS

or

FIVE TOYS that you'll only get to play with for ONE YEAR?

Go to the mall while cuddling lots of PUPPIES

or

Go to the park and play with DRAGONS?

Throw a SWIMMING POOL party

or

Play with a BIG TRAMPOLINE?

TIME FOR SCHOOL

Even brave heroes need to learn and get good grades!

Would you rather...

Be the best DANCER in your school

or

The best ATHLETE?

Wear a SUPERHERO CAPE to school

or

A PIRATE EYEPATCH to school?

Be elected CLASS PRESIDENT

or

Win a SOCCER award?

Stay up ALL NIGHT watching CARTOONS

or

SKIP SCHOOL for a day?

Be captain of the FOOTBALL team

or

Be captain of the DEBATE team?

Be genius level SMART

or

Have the most FRIENDS in school?

Have a cool TREEHOUSE in the school playground

or

Be able to play FORTNITE with your classmates at school?

Go to school wearing a CLOWN NOSE

or

Go to school wearing a CLOWN WIG?

Go to school riding the SCHOOL BUS

or

Go to school riding a DINOSAUR?

Eat food from the school CAFETERIA

or

PACK your own lunch?

Play FLAG-football

or

Play TACKLE-football?

Take an ART class

or

Take a MUSIC class?

NEVER have to do homework again

or

BE PAID to always do your homework?

Have MANY good friends

or

Have ONE best friend?

Lose five FRIENDS

or

Gain one ENEMY?

Give a 30-minute SPEECH in front of your ENTIRE school

or

WORK in your school CAFETERIA for one week?

Go home from school every day TO EAT LUNCH

or

Go home ONE HOUR EARLY every day?

Go to the PLAYGROUND eight times a month

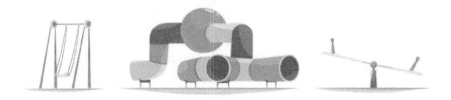

or

Go to an AMUSEMENT PARK just once a month?

Be the FUNNIEST person in class

or

Be the SMARTEST?

Remember everything you READ

or

Be able to solve any MATH problem?

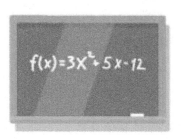

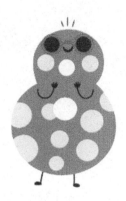

YOUR SECOND QUEST

Let's continue on in our journey with another DARE!

Would you rather...

Eat 100 BARs of chocolate

or

Drink 100 BOTTLEs of lemonade?

Get free CANDY from witches and wizards

or

Get free TOYS from elves and reindeer?

Wear your SHOES on the wrong feet

or

Wear your PANTS backwards?

Win a race on a BICYCLE

or

Win a race on a SCOOTER?

Jump off a DIVING BOARD

or

Go down a LONG TWISTY SLIDE?

Walk BACKWARDS to the next destination

or

Walk on your HANDS instead?

Spend a day SNEEZING every time you STAND up from a chair

or

Spend it HICCOUGHING every time you took a STEP?

Clean a giant's EARS

or

Clean a giant's NOSE?

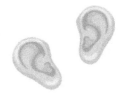

Swallow a MOSQUITO

or

Swallow a FLY?

Be covered in MUD for a week

or

Be covered in SLIME for a week?

Finish BOOGER-flavored ice cream

or

EARWAX-flavored ice cream?

HOP everywhere you go

or

WALK BACKWARDS everywhere you go?

Eat a BUG

or

Never eat CHOCOLATE again?

Lick the bottom of your SHOES

or

Eat your BOOGERS?

Always SAY OUT LOUD what's on your mind

or

NEVER speak again?

SING every time you talk

or

DANCE every time you move?

CARTWHEEL during the rest of the adventure

or

CRAWL ON ALL FOURS to get anywhere?

Wear only OVERSIZED clothes the rest of the journey

or

Wear only TIGHT clothes?

Spend a week CRYING when you hear something FUNNY

or

Spend it LAUGHING when you hear something SAD?

Say something FUNNY when someone asks a SERIOUS question

Say something SERIOUS when someone asks you a FUNNY question?

Spend the day as a TALL TREE

or

A PRETTY FLOWER?

Live without MUSIC

or

Live without VIDEO GAMES?

Stay stuck on a desert island ALONE

or

Stay stuck on a desert island WITH YOUR WORST ENEMY?

Search for a hidden piggy bank that DOUBLES any money you put in

or

Find a fairy that will leave $10 under your pillow every morning?

VICTORY! LET'S FEAST!

Hooray, you made it! It's time to celebrate!

Would you rather...

Have a magical glass that never runs out of SODA

or

Have a magical bowl that never runs out of POPCORN?

Eat with CHOPSTICKS

or

Eat with your BARE HANDS?

Eat a CHOCOLATE BAR

or

Get a LOLLIPOP?

Eat an entire CAKE

or

An entire tub of ICE CREAM?

Eat extra-SPICY spaghetti

or

Eat extra-SWEET spaghetti?

Eat a bag of CHIPS

or

Eat a box of COOKIES?

Eat only HAMBURGERS

or

Eat only HOTDOGS?

Eat everything with a SPOON

or

Eat everything with a FORK?

Eat an entire loaf of BREAD

or

Eat a whole basket of FRUITS?

Eat an entire glass of KETCHUP

or

An entire glass of MUSTARD?

Drink a glass of KOOL-AID

or

Drink a glass of CHOCOLATE MILK?

Eat some SPAGHETTI

or

Eat some TACOS?

Eat a whole LEMON

or

Eat a whole RAW POTATO?

Eat PIZZA every day for a year

or

Eat ICE CREAM every day for a year?

Get an unlimited supply of CHOCOLATE

or

Get an unlimited supply of FRUIT PUNCH?

Eat COOKIE DOUGH

or

Eat CHOCOLATE BROWNIE BATTER?

Drink a teaspoon of VINEGAR

or

Drink a teaspoon of HOT SAUCE?

Not EAT for a day

or

Not DRINK for a day?

Eat a HAMBURGER for BREAKFAST

or

Eat CEREAL for DESSERT?

Eat POPSICLES

or

Eat ICE CREAM CONES?

Have unlimited COOKIES

or

Have unlimited PIZZA?

Drink from a BOWL all the time

or

From a BABY BOTTLE?

Drink MAGIC POTION

or

Eat LEVITATING PUDDING?

Dip your face into a plate of VINEGAR

or

Into a plate of BBQ SAUCE?

Eat CAKE dipped in KETCHUP

or

Eat MEATLOAF dipped in CHOCOLATE?

Eat a dozen DOUGHNUTS in one sitting

or

Eat a dozen COOKIES in one sitting?

Eat only PIZZA for the rest of your life

or

Eat only FRENCH FRIES for the rest of your life?

Drink a glass of GARLIC JUICE

or

A glass of ONION JUICE?

Eat a bowl of JELLY BEANS

or

A bowl of GUMMY BEARS?

Eat STRAWBERRIES dipped in MAYONNAISE

or

Eat APPLES dipped in SALT?

Eat a banana sandwich with SOY SAUCE

or

Eat a banana sandwich with KETCHUP?

Eat only ASPARAGUS for the rest of your life

or

Eat only BRUSSEL SPROUTS for the rest of your life?

Eat a bowl of SPAGHETTI SAUCE without NOODLES

or

Eat a bowl of NOODLES without SAUCE?

Eat FISH-FLAVORED cookies

or

Eat GARLIC-FLAVORED ice cream?

Give up eating SWEETS

or

Give up eating FAST FOOD?

OFF TO THE FUTURE

What a wonderful adventure! Now off to dreaming about your NEXT journey.

Would you rather...

Be a famous INVENTOR

or

Be a famous WRITER?

Be a super-fast SWIMMER

or

Be a super-fast RUNNER?

Be a DENTIST

or

Be a DOCTOR?

Be a famous SINGER

or

Be a famous ACTOR/ACTRESS?

Win a GOLD OLYMPIC MEDAL

Or

Win A MILLION DOLLARS?

Be a FIREMAN

or

Be a POLICEMAN?

Be a BALLERINA

or

Be a GYMNAST?

Be a SCIENTIST

or

Be a BRAIN SURGEON?

Be a famous YOUTUBER

or

Be the SMARTEST PERSON in the world?

Be a DETECTIVE

or

Be THE NEXT PRESIDENT?

Be a BOWLING champion

or

Be a HOCKEY champion?

Be RICH and UGLY

or

Be POOR and GOOD-LOOKING?

Be with your TRUE LOVE

or

Be a MILLIONAIRE?

Be a brave SOLDIER

or

Be an amazing TEACHER?

Be a famous MAGICIAN

or

Be a talented CIRCUS PERFORMER?

Be a LION TAMER

or

Be a BEAR TRAINER?

Find the CURE to a deadly ILLNESS

or

Find the END to WORLD HUNGER?

Be a famous ACTOR

or

Be a famous CHEF?

Be the RICHEST person in the world

or

Be the KINDEST person in the world?

THE MOST TREASURED CUSTOMER YOU!

The Laughing Lion hopes you enjoyed the book!

As the Lion was writing it, he imagined how happy you'd be with the finished book.
How you'd jump for joy when you received it in the post.
How you'd write in your journal that it's the best book on the planet!
How you'd pass it onto your children for generations to come.

If you did enjoy the book, please take 20 seconds to leave a review.

The Laughing Lion loves reading all the happy moments his books spark.

Wishing you many more joyous moments!

Laughing Lion

Made in the USA
Monee, IL
17 December 2020